GH00976344

Please take great care of this book, protect it in bad weather and handle it only with clean hands.

Return it on or before the last date stamped below. If you want the book again, ask the librarian to renew it.

- 4 JUN 2009

2 4 OCT 2009

2 4 OCT 2010

3 1 AUG 2015

YOU ARE RESPONSIBLE FOR THE SAFE RETURN
OF THIS BOOK IN GOOD CONDITION

PLEASE BRING YOUR TICKET TO THE LIBRARY EVERY TIME
YOU BORROW OR RENEW   LIB.39 05/02

EALING LIBRARIES www.ealing.gov.uk

11 696 636 0

Pope BENEDICT XVI

Pope
BENEDICT XVI

Tom Streissguth

Twenty-First Century Books
Minneapolis

London Borough of Ealing Library & Information Service	
11 696 636 0	
PETERS	01-Oct-07
£13.99	CEN
J282.092ben	

BIOGRAPHY is a trademark of A&E Television Networks. All rights reserved.

Some of the people profiled in this series have also been featured in the acclaimed BIOGRAPHY® series, on The Biography Channel®, which is available on DVD from A&E Home Video. ShopAETV.com.

Copyright © 2007 by Tom Streissguth

All rights reserved. International copyright secured. No part of this book may be reproduced, stored in a retrieval system, or transmitted in any form or by any means—electronic, mechanical, photocopying, recording, or otherwise—without the prior written permission of Lerner Publishing Group, except for the inclusion of brief quotations in an acknowledged review.

Twenty-First Century Books
A division of Lerner Publishing Group
241 First Avenue North
Minneapolis, MN 55401 U.S.A.

Website addresses: www.lernerbooks.com
www.biography.com

Library of Congress Cataloging-in-Publication Data

Streissguth, Thomas, 1958–
 Pope Benedict XVI / by Tom Streissguth.
  p. cm. — (Biography)
 Includes bibliographical references and index.
 ISBN-13: 978–0–8225–5952–8 (lib. bdg. : alk. paper)
 ISBN-10: 0–8225–5952–8 (lib. bdg. : alk. paper)
  1. Benedict XVI, Pope, 1927– 2. Popes—Biography. I. Title. II. A&E
 biography (Twenty-First Century Books (Firm))
 BX1378.6.S77 2007
 282.092—dc22   2005032824

Manufactured in the United States of America
1 2 3 4 5 6 – BP – 12 11 10 09 08 07

CONTENTS

Joseph Cardinal Ratzinger (center) *presides over the funeral of Pope John Paul II in Vatican City.*

INTRODUCTION

In the early evening of April 2, 2005, Pope John Paul II lay dying in his private apartment. Eduardo Cardinal Somalo moved toward the pope's bed. He called out the pope's name three times, then listened carefully for a response.

This ritual had taken place for centuries, in the last moments of hundreds of popes. Somalo heard nothing. He saw that John Paul II had died. The pope had reigned over the Catholic Church for twenty-eight years.

Soon afterward, Archbishop Leonardo Sandri appeared on the steps of the Basilica of Saint Peter. This cathedral lies at the center of the Vatican, the headquarters of the Catholic Church. Sandri prepared to announce Pope John Paul's death to the world.

Cardinal Somalo served as camerlengo, the "chamberlain" of the Holy Roman Church. His duty was to make sure of the pope's death. He would then call for a conclave, an important meeting that the entire world would be carefully watching. Catholic cardinals from all over the world would soon be coming to Rome to choose the next pope.

A FAREWELL TO THE POPE

In the last years of his reign, Pope John Paul II had appeared before millions of people, even as his health was failing. He had difficulty walking. His hands often shook. Sometimes he could not speak above a whisper. But he had carried on his many duties. They included presiding at church ceremonies, giving homilies (short religious lessons), saying Mass, and encouraging the faithful.

When Pope John Paul II's voice had been silenced, the entire world seemed to mourn. Bells rang at the Vatican and all over the city of Rome. Millions of pilgrims arrived in Rome, the capital of Italy, to pay their respects to the pope who had served them so well. On April 8, the day of the funeral, more than half a million people packed Saint Peter's Square at the Vatican. Among them were kings, presidents, ambassadors, prime ministers, priests, and members of many religions.

During the funeral, an elderly cardinal rose to give a short sermon. Joseph Cardinal Ratzinger described the life of John Paul II, who had been born Karol Wojtyla. Ratzinger recounted the pope's youth in Poland. He described his experiences during World War II (1939–1945), when Nazi Germany had occupied Poland. He described the pope's life as a priest and as archbishop of Krakow, a devoutly Catholic city in Poland. He talked of the pope's election in 1978 and his many trips to foreign nations. He had inspired people, Catholics and non-Catholics, around the world. To the millions watching, Cardinal Ratzinger announced, "We can be sure that our beloved Pope is standing today at the window of the Father's house, that he sees us and blesses us."

Cardinal Ratzinger had been a close friend of the pope. He held one of the highest positions in the church. Many even thought he would be a good candidate to succeed John Paul II. But the choice of a new pope was not going to be easy. Some people in the church wanted a non-European. Cardinal Ratzinger was from Germany. Others wanted someone who understood new ways of thinking about the rules and doctrines of the church. Cardinal Ratzinger thought the old-fashioned beliefs and rules were still best. Although he didn't like controversy, Ratzinger had argued in many debates. In the days to come, he would find himself in the middle of another debate. He and his peers would decide on a new leader for the Catholic Church. At the end of the debate, this quiet man would find himself thrust into public life in one of the most powerful positions in the world. He would become pope and spiritual leader of one billion Catholics worldwide.

Joseph was born in this house in Marktl am Inn, Germany, in 1927.

Chapter **ONE**

A YOUTH IN GERMANY

THE LITTLE TOWN OF MARKTL AM INN LIES ALONG the Inn River in eastern Bavaria. Nearby is the border between Germany and Austria. Marktl has only 2,700 inhabitants. But, like many small towns of Europe, its history goes back to medieval times. The tall white steeple of the Church of Saint Oswald, a symbol of the people's devout Catholic faith, rises over the old marketplace.

In the center of Marktl, at 11 Schulstrasse, stands a traditional Bavarian house with a pitched roof, wooden shutters, and whitewashed walls. Here, Joseph Alois Ratzinger was born on April 16, 1927. His father, Joseph, was a police officer. His mother, Maria, worked as a cook. Joseph was the youngest of three children. He had an older brother, Georg, and a sister, Maria.

The Ratzinger family, like many others in Germany, was going through hard times. Nearly ten years after its defeat in World War I (1914–1918), Germany was still in an economic depression. The Treaty of Versailles, signed after the war, had set down harsh terms. The treaty forced Germany to admit responsibility for starting the war. Germany had to reduce its military to one hundred thousand men. It also had to pay reparations, an enormous sum of money for war damages.

The reparations ruined the German economy. The government had no money. Goods and food became expensive. Many companies went out of business. Work was scarce, with millions unemployed. Joseph Ratzinger held his job, although he had to move the family from place to place. In 1929 the Ratzingers moved to Tittmoning, on the Salzach River. Three years later, they moved to Aschau am Inn, a small farm town, where they lived in an apartment above police headquarters.

A strong faith in the Catholic Church helped the family through these hard times. Every Sunday the Ratzingers walked to church to attend Mass. In this ceremony, Catholics take part in Holy Communion, the sharing of consecrated (blessed) bread and wine, which is believed to be the body and blood of Jesus Christ. The devotion of the Ratzingers was typical of families in Bavaria, where Catholicism was strong. The nearby town of Altotting held a famous shrine to the Virgin Mary. It had attracted pilgrims (worshippers) for more than one thousand years. Other shrines and roadside crosses had been erected all over Bavaria.

The church and its ceremonies inspired young Joseph Ratzinger. He joyously celebrated the holidays of Christmas and Easter. He studied the Bible and the German prayer book. He wondered at the beauty of the Mass, spoken in Latin, the ancient language of the early Church. When he was five years old, Joseph met Michael Cardinal Faulhaber of Munich. After this encounter, the boy dreamed of entering the church and becoming a cardinal himself.

DEFYING THE NAZI PARTY

But the church was also coming under attack from a politician who had no interest in religion. Adolf Hitler was from Braunau, a town just a few miles from Marktl. He had fought in World War I. During the war, Hitler had been temporarily blinded by a poison gas attack. The surrender of Germany had left him a broken, bitter man. He felt deep rage and frustration at Germany's humiliation, at the Treaty of Versailles, and at his own poverty. Hitler gathered followers by speaking out against the treaty and the new government of Germany. He also joined the tiny National Socialist (Nazi) Party. The Nazis called for a stronger central government. They also wanted to see Germany's military and economic power grow strong again. Hitler attracted many new members to the party's ranks. He promised to rebuild the German army, and to stop reparations. In 1933 the party won the national elections. President Paul von Hindenburg then appointed Hitler as the new chancellor, the most powerful job in the German government. Hitler quickly began making the changes that he had promised.

The elder Joseph Ratzinger strongly opposed Hitler and the Nazi Party. He realized that the Nazis wanted to weaken the church and make people loyal to Hitler and his ideas instead. But Ratzinger was taking a dangerous stand. Hitler was threatening all those who disagreed with him. He was also threatening Jews. He blamed the Jews for Germany's defeat in World War I. Ratzinger spoke out against the Nazis in meetings with his colleagues and in public. He found that few people agreed with him—or had enough courage to agree.

Soon after the Nazis came to power, they began running Germany as a police state. Only one political party—the Nazi Party—was allowed. Those who publicly disagreed with the party were imprisoned. Nazi brownshirts assaulted opponents in the streets. (Brownshirts were uniformed party members.) In 1935 all German men between the ages of eighteen and forty-five became army reservists. The government could call them up at any time to train and fight in the German army.

Hitler also took steps against Germany's churches. He felt a strong contempt for Christianity. He saw this faith as foreign to Germany, imposed on its people from outside. (Missionaries had converted Germans to Christianity after the fall of the Roman Empire in the fifth century A.D.) Hitler saw the old German gods as Germany's true national religion. He saw in the Germanic gods, such as Wotan and Thor, symbols of strength, loyalty, and honor. In his opinion, these were better values for his nation than the mercy and charity preached by Jesus Christ.

The Catholic Church, Hitler believed, also stood in the way of creating a new order in Germany. The Nazis

HITLER'S CHURCH

For Adolf Hitler and the Nazi Party, the Catholic Church and all other churches posed a threat and a challenge. Hitler expected undivided loyalty to the Third Reich, or Nazi empire. He believed that faith in God and trust in church leaders would turn people against his regime.

For this reason, the Nazis created the Reichskirche (Reich Church) in 1934. The Nazi government organized and controlled this church. The crucifix, a cross that depicts the crucified Jesus, was replaced by the swastika, the symbol of Hitler's state. The Bible was removed from the service. The Reichskirche replaced the Bible with *Mein Kampf*, or "My Struggle." In *Mein Kampf*, Hitler described his life and his plans for Germany. Only Nazi Party officials with special invitations could preach sermons in the Reichskirche. They praised the ideals of party and state rather than the Christian ideals of charity and mercy.

banned Catholic newspapers. They vandalized churches and broke into religious offices. The Nazis also attacked priests in the streets and in their homes. The government then banned all Catholic trade unions (organized labor groups). In 1935 the party arrested several priests and accused them of immoral acts. They put the priests on trial to humiliate them. Newspapers, all under the control of the Nazis, covered the trials with big headlines. The church was publicly shamed.

In 1937 Pope Pius XI wrote the encyclical *With Burning Sorrow*. The encyclical was a letter to the archbishops and bishops of the church. It condemned the anti-Catholic acts taking place in Germany. The pope also harshly condemned Nazi godlessness. *With Burning Sorrow* circulated underground (secretly) throughout Germany. In hundreds of churches, priests read out the pope's words and commands from their pulpits.

THE HITLER YOUTH

Hitler and the Nazis were also taking steps against Catholic schools. Party officials threatened parents for enrolling their children in these schools. The Nazis shut down some Catholic schools by force. Nazi Party members and brownshirts invaded their offices and destroyed their files. They padlocked the doors and removed priests, teachers, and students from the schools. In the face of threats of violence, many priests and nuns left the church. The Nazis rewarded them with well-paid jobs.

Hitler believed everyone in Germany should belong to the Nazi Party. The party would replace Catholic youth groups or any other group that did not totally support Nazism. To that end, the Nazis organized the Hitlerjugend (Hitler Youth) and the Bund Deutscher Madel (League of German Girls). In 1938 Hitler required all boys and girls to join these groups. During the same year, Georg Ratzinger entered Saint Michael's, a Catholic seminary (school for religious training) in Traunstein. He also joined the Hitler Youth. In 1939 Joseph Ratzinger followed his elder brother to Saint Michael's.

Boys in the Hitler Youth and girls in the League of German Girls stand on stage during a meeting in the 1940s. Georg and Joseph Ratzinger were members because they were required to join.

The two brothers lived and worked with about sixty other students at the seminary. Their day began at 5:00 A.M., followed by Mass at 6:30. They attended classes in the morning, followed by study in the afternoon. Joseph enjoyed learning the classical languages of Greek and Latin. The authors of the Bible's New Testament had written in Greek. Catholics celebrated Mass in Latin. The pope also used Latin when writing his instructions and encyclicals. Joseph took great pride and pleasure in his work. He enjoyed nothing so much as reading books and studying.

Left to right: *Joseph, Georg, their mother Maria, sister Maria, and their father Joseph Ratzinger in 1938*

Joseph didn't mind the school's many strict rules. For many others his age, the church seemed a dreary, ancient institution that only told them what *not* to do. But for Joseph, Catholicism made life easy and joyful. He took great pleasure in reading the Bible and studying the life of Christ. The Catholic faith gave him comfort in a time when hatred and greed for power were taking control of Germany.

His father, in the meantime, had retired from the police force. He was sixty years old and out of favor in the police force because of his opposition to the Nazis. Seeking a quiet life in the countryside, he moved his family to Hufschlag, near the city of Traunstein. The family lived in a farmhouse on land that Joseph Ratzinger had bought in 1933.

With his two sons in a seminary, Joseph Ratzinger took pride in the thought that Georg and Joseph might someday become priests. He could have planned no better future for them. But with the Nazis in power, the future was uncertain.

Adolf Hitler speaks to a crowd in 1941 to rally support for the Nazi cause.

Chapter **TWO**

THE WAR

ON SEPTEMBER 1, 1939, ADOLF HITLER ORDERED the German army into Poland. France and Britain—the Allies—then declared war on Germany. German tanks rolled across the fields of western Poland. At the same time, the Red Army of the Soviet Union (a group of Communist states, including Russia) invaded from the east. Just before the start of the war, Germany and the Soviet Union had secretly agreed to attack and divide Polish territory. Poland's small army fought bravely but had no chance of defending the country. World War II had begun in Europe.

In the next year, Germany invaded France, Belgium, Denmark, the Netherlands, and Norway. Hitler's powerful armies achieved easy victories. The Nazis occupied much of Europe. They arrested anyone who opposed them. German army and police units also rounded up Jews and sent them to huge concentration (prison) camps. There, the Nazis used the Jewish prisoners as slave labor or murdered them.

In Traunstein and throughout Germany, all young people turning fourteen years of age had to join the Hitler Youth. The headmaster of the Traunstein seminary saw to it that all fourteen-year-old boys—including Joseph Ratzinger—joined. The headmaster may have feared that the Nazi government would close down the seminary if this rule were not obeyed. But despite the headmaster's actions, the German army took over the seminary in 1942. The army turned it into a military hospital. Joseph Ratzinger moved out of the seminary. He began attending the Maximilians Gymnasium, the public high school in Traunstein.

Membership in the Hitler Youth meant attending meetings and training camps to prepare for Nazi Party membership. At first, Ratzinger went, unwillingly, to meetings. After a short while, he stopped. By doing so, he risked the loss of an important privilege—a reduction in the fee his family had to pay the school. A sympathetic math teacher helped him by faking a certificate of attendance. Joseph Ratzinger believed it was useless, and certainly dangerous, to openly defy the Nazis. But he could never replace his Catholic faith with loyalty to a political party. He would do only what he had to do and wait for the war to end.

KAROL WOJTYLA'S WAR

After the German invasion of Poland in 1939, a young Polish student named Karol Wojtyla found his life disrupted and in danger. The Jagiellonian University, which he was attending in the Polish city of Krakow, shut down. The German occupiers also closed all churches and banned the Catholic Mass. Determined to carry on his studies, Wojtyla attended an underground seminary in Krakow. For this, he could have been arrested and put in a prison camp. To escape the Germans, he took refuge in the home of the archbishop of Krakow.

Soon after the end of the war in 1945, Wojtyla was ordained as a priest. The Catholic Church had been an important focus of resistance during the war. It also resisted Communism after the war, when a Communist regime took power in Poland. Wojtyla's devotion to his faith made him a hero to Polish Catholics. They attended Mass despite the government's ban on religion. The church rewarded Wojtyla's efforts by electing him Pope John Paul II in 1978.

MEMBER OF THE FLAK

The tide of the war turned against Germany in 1942. In that year, Hitler ordered the invasion of the Soviet Union. German armies marched as far as the gates of Moscow, the capital of the Soviet Union. The Soviet army and the brutally cold Russian winter turned them back. As soldiers fell to battle deaths and illness, the German army replaced them with more young men. Joseph Ratzinger's turn came in 1943. The German army drafted him and other members of his class into the antiaircraft corps, known as the FLAK. These units used artillery to battle enemy bombers from the ground. Ratzinger went through training in Munich, the capital of Bavaria. FLAK officers then put him to work building antiaircraft defenses at a factory near the city. He constructed large emplacements (pits) in the ground for the guns. Then he loaded sandbags to surround the emplacements. When a factory that his unit was protecting was destroyed, his unit moved to a new position. Meanwhile, he attended school when he could, often reading and working well into the night.

On September 10, 1944, the FLAK released Ratzinger. When he returned home, he found another draft notice. This time he had to join the Reichsarbeitsdienst, the national labor service. Members of these units repaired buildings, roads, train tracks—whatever had been damaged by the war. They also helped build defensive positions. Ratzinger joined a truck convoy to the Hungarian border of Austria. There, he helped dig trenches and emplacements to slow down enemy tanks.

Germany was calling on anyone who could lift a shovel to help prepare for an attack by its enemies. The Nazi government issued guns to old men and boys. Then it ordered them into the trenches. While German units were in retreat, the Soviet army was marching through Hungary toward Austria. U.S. units (which had joined the war in 1941) were driving across southern Germany from the west. By 1945 it was clear that Germany's once-powerful army was beaten. The war would soon be lost.

The country fell into confusion as German soldiers and families desperately tried to escape the fighting, air raids, and starvation. Adolf Hitler, once the master of Europe, took shelter in a small underground bunker in the German capital of Berlin. On April 30, while enemy units drove into the city, Hitler killed himself. In these final days, Joseph Ratzinger threw off his uniform and deserted the army. He defied the order that had come down from the Nazi high command: the people of Traunstein must fight to the last person. On May 7, Germany officially surrendered. The war in Europe had ended.

After World War II, Soviet armies occupied Eastern Europe and northeastern Germany. The Soviet Union put new Communist governments in place. East Germany became a Communist state, in which private property was banned and a single political party ruled. West Germany remained democratic, allied to the Western European nations and the United States. Communist parties also ruled in Poland and other Eastern European countries. The new governments saw the Catholic Church as a rival for the loyalty of the people. Communist regimes forced priests out of their posts. The regimes also closed down the churches and banned religious services. In much of Eastern Europe, the faithful held Mass in secret.

A STUDENT OF THEOLOGY

U.S. troops occupied Traunstein soon after Joseph Ratzinger deserted his post. The Americans were taking many adult men and teenagers as prisoners. They captured Ratzinger and marched him for three days to a prisoner-of-war camp near the city of Ulm. The prisoners slept in the open, on both clear and rainy nights. Ratzinger spent his days talking with the other prisoners and writing his thoughts in a small notebook. Priests who had also been taken prisoner celebrated Mass on Sundays. Ratzinger attended faithfully.

On June 19, after checking Ratzinger's background, the camp commander presented him with a certificate that officially released him. Ratzinger boarded a truck bound for Munich. From there he hitchhiked and walked back to Traunstein. The war was over. He was

After the war, Joseph Ratzinger moved to the Georgianum (above), a university near Munich, to study theology.

again a free man. At eighteen years of age, he had some important decisions to make.

That summer Joseph and Georg returned to their seminary. The military hospital had closed, and the staff had moved patients elsewhere. The Ratzinger sons helped restore the dormitories and classrooms. In the fall, they went to Freising. There, they entered another seminary that would be their last place of study for the priesthood. Under his prefect (instructor), Alfred Lapple, Joseph studied important works of philosophy and theology (the study of religious history and ideas). He read the works of Saint Augustine, a fifth-century bishop. Augustine described the church's proper place in the world and the way Christians should conduct their public and private lives. Ratzinger learned from the works of Saint Thomas Aquinas, a medieval philosopher and scientist. He also read the works of the nineteenth-century writer Friedrich Nietzsche. This German philosopher believed the world was moving into a new era, in which men and women would lose their faith and abandon religion altogether.

In 1947 Ratzinger began his studies at the Georgianum, a university of theology. The Georgianum, near the city of Munich, took up the grounds and buildings of an old castle. Students slept in unheated halls. Classes were held inside a large greenhouse, where plants were sheltered from the cold. Ratzinger did not mind the cramped rooms, uncomfortable conditions, or hard work. The study of ideas—whether those of a Christian or an atheist, a Saint Augustine or a Friedrich Nietzsche—fascinated him. The difficult books and articles he studied made him realize that learning could be a never-ending discovery and challenge, the work of a lifetime.

The Bible itself was a vast and tangled mystery. For two thousand years, scholars had been arguing over who wrote it and what historical events inspired it. The Georgianum professors gave many lectures on the Bible. Each professor offered his own ideas. The students sometimes challenged these ideas with theories of their own. They had to defend their ideas in long, carefully written essays.

In this scholarly hothouse, Ratzinger realized that professors could be as combative and competitive, in their own way, as athletes or soldiers. He witnessed many intellectual battles among his teachers and fellow students. In the background loomed the pope and the Vatican. One of the Vatican's many roles was to supervise the writing of church officials on the subject of the Bible and the Catholic faith. The Vatican disciplined those writers who did not follow accepted church thinking. A theology professor who held to wrong ideas could lose his position. He could see his scholarly career come to an abrupt end.

In 1949 the Georgianum moved to the city of Munich. For the next two years, Joseph worked hard to prepare himself for his ordination—the ceremony that would officially make him a Catholic priest. In the summer of 1950, he took and passed the final examination at the Georgianum. But his work was just beginning. To become a priest, he had to memorize the liturgy, the proper words and actions, for Mass, baptism, marriage, funerals, and other religious ceremonies. He wrote sermons and studied the proper ways to teach the Bible. Ratzinger enjoyed this endless hard work. There was so much tradition and knowledge in the Catholic Church. And he wanted to know it all.

MEMBER OF THE PRIESTHOOD

The day Joseph Ratzinger had been waiting for nearly all his life finally came on June 29, 1951. Cardinal

Joseph Ratzinger (right), *his brother Georg* (left), *and a friend* (center) *on the day of their ordination in Freising in 1951*

Faulhaber ordained Ratzinger and his brother Georg as priests in the cathedral at Freising. Soon afterward the brothers said their first Mass to the people of their hometown in the Church of Saint Oswald in Traunstein.

As a young priest, Father Joseph Ratzinger had to serve where the church directed him. The diocese (a territory under the authority of a bishop) appointed him as the assistant pastor at the Precious Blood parish of Munich. He soon discovered that the schedule of a priest was very demanding. His many duties took his attention seven days a week. He could be called to perform them at any time of the day or night. Ratzinger led Mass, presided at weddings and funerals, and heard confessions. In this private conversation with members of the church, Ratzinger heard faithful Catholics confess their sins. He guided them on proper conduct and absolved (forgave) them in the name of Jesus Christ.

Still, Ratzinger did not give up his studies. He attended the University of Munich, reading the works of Saint Augustine. He won a prize with his thesis (a long and detailed essay) on Augustine. The university accepted this paper as a doctoral dissertation, an original work of research. This qualified Ratzinger for the highest degree he could attain in the study of theology. Ratzinger officially received the title Doctor of Theology in July 1953.

At the same time, he was working on a thesis about Saint Bonaventure, an early church leader. If accepted,

A *sculpture of Saint Bonaventure, the subject of Ratzinger's thesis*

this thesis would qualify him as a full professor of theology. He read everything he could find on Saint Bonaventure. He also lectured at the College for Philosophy and Theology in Freising.

For this work, the sailing was not so smooth. Father Ratzinger had trouble working and teaching at the same time. He was also worrying about his parents, who were growing old and frail. In the fall of 1955, Father Ratzinger and his siblings helped his parents to move from the country to a house in Traunstein. There, they could easily get around.

After moving his parents, Ratzinger finished his paper on Saint Bonaventure. He turned it in to two elder scholars. They would read and grade it. More trouble came up when one of the readers rejected the thesis. He criticized Father Ratzinger for not presenting his ideas clearly enough and for ignoring the work of other scholars who had written on the same subject. Ratzinger would have to rewrite his thesis and turn it in again.

He set to work immediately. He removed several chapters of the thesis. He rewrote and expanded oth-

The Ratzinger family in the early 1950s (left to right), Maria, Georg, their mother, Joseph, and their father

ers. He answered the many questions and criticisms of his paper. After only two weeks of work, he turned it in again. This time the readers passed his written work. Father Ratzinger then had to meet with the two scholars to defend his work and answer any questions. He succeeded.

Ratzinger then became a professor of theology at the Freising Superior School of Philosophy and Theology. In 1958 he was invited to teach at the University of Bonn. He accepted this appointment, even though it meant a move away from his hometown and from his parents. His brother Georg moved to Traunstein, however. That eased Joseph's fears of leaving his mother and father alone.

Father Ratzinger didn't realize it yet, but with his success as a scholar would come more hard work and difficulties. Although he loved the life of a scholar, he now had to take up a position on the academic battlefield. The ideas of scholars would clash. Bitter debates would take place. And Ratzinger would argue over the Catholic faith and the future of the church. It was a new scene, with new people. And it was very far from Traunstein and the quiet life he had known.

The Basilica of Saint Martin in Bonn, Germany, near the University of Bonn, where Joseph Ratzinger taught Catholic theology from 1959 to 1963. Many people stopped going to church after the grief and horror of World War II.

Chapter **THREE**

THE CHURCH IN A CHANGING WORLD

AFTER THE END OF WORLD WAR II IN **1945,** THE church in Germany quickly recovered from Nazi persecution. But throughout Europe, faith and interest in religion was fading. Fewer people attended Mass. And many churches stood empty, even on Sundays. The great medieval cathedrals that soared over the old town centers attracted more tourists than worshippers.

Many of those who still attended church questioned its ideas and rules. The church seemed to many to be just a big bureaucracy, or policy-making group. Its popes, cardinals, bishops, and priests seemed interested only in guarding their privileges. At one time, many Catholics had taken vows of poverty, chastity, and charity. They had spent their lives in meditation and worship. In the bustling twentieth century, very few Catholics led this traditional life.

Catholics also questioned the church's guidance of their private lives. The Catholic Church still forbade divorce. Married couples were expected to respect their marriage vows and stay together until death, no matter what. The church also encouraged large families and prohibited the use of birth control. Although some Catholics obeyed, others did not. They saw their private lives as their own business and not that of a priest, bishop, or distant pope.

The church also had to decide its proper role in the modern world. Was the Catholic Church only concerned with religion? Or should it have something to say about politics, economics, justice, and poverty? Should it attempt to gain new converts? Should it accept other faiths as equally important and valid? What stand should it take on other Christian sects (groups) that did not accept the authority of the pope? Should the pope and the Vatican remain the voice of absolute authority over all Catholics?

The church had to answer these questions. If not, Catholicism might become a relic of history, a forgotten faith. The chance to modernize the Catholic faith came with the election of Pope John XXIII in 1958. In the next year, the pope announced that the Vatican would hold a general meeting of the church. It would be the first since the Vatican Council of 1869. The bishops would gather in Rome and discuss the many modern problems facing the church. They would try to settle the tough questions and agree on the proper church doctrine for the future. This Second Vatican Council, or Vatican II, would be the most important event in the church in centuries.

FATHER RATZINGER AND THE VATICAN COUNCIL

In 1959 Joseph Ratzinger moved to Bonn, the capital of West Germany. He was a full professor at the

Father Ratzinger taught theology at the university in Bonn, West Germany (above).

University of Bonn, giving lectures on Catholic theology. As a scholar and teacher, he was a success. His fellow professors respected his writing. And his students filled the halls for his lectures. He also liked Bonn. In this bustling city, he could attend concerts and visit a museum dedicated to composer Ludwig van Beethoven (1770–1827). Beethoven had been born in this city. Ratzinger made friends with many famous scholars. He had known them only by name while he was growing up.

Father Ratzinger's fame as a scholar spread. His name became familiar to Catholic priests and theology students all over the world. For the Second Vatican Council, a German cardinal, Joseph Frings, called on Ratzinger to serve as a *peritus,* an expert on theology. It would be Ratzinger's job to advise Cardinal Frings and other bishops and cardinals on how the church had decided important issues in the past.

For two years, from 1960 to 1962, Ratzinger prepared for the great council. He studied the history of the church. He read about the councils of the past, particularly the Council of Trent, which took place in the mid-sixteenth century. The Council of Trent helped the church to meet the challenge of the Protestant Reformation. The Protestants had questioned the authority of the pope and of Catholic leaders. In the twentieth century, the church was again facing challenges to its authority. It faced the issues of social justice, poverty, morality, war, individual rights to privacy

The Vatican (above) *is the center of the Roman Catholic Church and the home of the pope. It is a separate country within the city of Rome, Italy.*

in sexual matters, and the degree of participation by church members in deciding church matters.

In the fall of 1962, the Second Vatican Council opened. Father Ratzinger and Cardinal Frings traveled to Rome. Frings saw Vatican II as a good chance to make changes in the church. He wanted to reform the Vatican's big bureaucracy. He felt determined, and he had influence in the church. But he was also elderly and nearly blind. Father Ratzinger would serve as the eyes and ears of Cardinal Frings. Ratzinger read through the documents and made summaries for the cardinal. He also helped him write his speeches and papers.

Pope Paul VI opens the second session of the Second Vatican Council in September 1963.

The Second Vatican Council officially opened for business on October 11. The pope presided over a ceremony welcoming 2,540 priests, bishops, and cardinals to Rome. For several months every fall for the next four years, these officials debated nearly every detail of their faith. They wrote documents, met in committees, and voted yes or no to the ideas expressed.

Father Ratzinger's life was divided between Germany and Rome. Back home, he joined the University of Munster in western Germany, where he taught for two years. He had the respect of his peers and students. But it was a hard time of difficult work, travel, and sadness in his family. On December 16, 1963, his mother died from cancer.

In Rome Ratzinger lived among other German-speaking priests and bishops. He gave lectures, led discussions, studied, wrote, and argued. Every detail of the faith was up for discussion and, if necessary, change. Even using Latin as the language of the Mass was under debate.

THE LANGUAGE OF THE CHURCH

An important issue for Joseph Ratzinger has always been language. By tradition, the Catholic Mass is said in Latin, the language of ancient Rome. After the crucifixion of Jesus Christ, apostles (Christ's followers) spread the Christian faith throughout the Roman Empire. For many years, Christians were banned and prosecuted by the Roman emperors. Christians went underground, celebrating Mass and writing in their native language of Latin. Many of the most important books of Christian theology first appeared in that language. Latin survived for centuries after the fall of Rome in A.D. 476 as the language of scholars as well as of the church. Latin words have survived in the writing of the church until modern times.

In the 1960s, Latin was rarely spoken outside the Catholic Church. After the Second Vatican Council, Latin began to disappear from Catholicism as well. A new liturgy, the Novus Ordo, was set down by Pope Paul VI. In most Catholic churches, modern languages that are understood by everyone celebrating Mass are used. This change upset many scholars, church officials, and some members of congregations. They thought the church was forgetting its history and traditions.

For Father Ratzinger, these were all positive events. He believed that the Vatican bureaucracy needed to change. In particular, in his view, the Sacred Congregation of the Holy Office had to change. The Holy Office was the largest department of the Vatican. It defended Catholic doctrine and punished those who broke the rules of the church. It banned certain books. It punished priests and bishops who fell out of line with church teaching. In the past, the Holy Office had been known as the Inquisition. It had tried people it accused of heresy (defiance of church authority). It turned some of these heretics over to town authorities for a public execution.

In Ratzinger's view, the Holy Office was out of step with modern times. It should have a new role, guiding and advising instead of punishing. He believed that the Vatican should allow more freedom to priests and bishops all over the world. The pope and the Curia—the Vatican government—should no longer have such power over local parishes. The Holy Office should inspire respect, not fear.

REVELATION

Another important issue for the Second Vatican Council was revelation—the appearance of God on Earth, among human beings. Father Ratzinger was a leading scholar on the subject of divine revelation. His treatise on Saint Bonaventure had explored this very subject. For this reason, Cardinal Frings assigned Father

THE INQUISITION

Since its early days in ancient Rome, the Catholic Church has dealt with heresies—teachings that go against the accepted doctrine (beliefs) of the church. To enforce its doctrines, the church set up an Episcopal Inquisition in the twelfth century. In the next century, the Papal Inquisition opened for business. These offices appointed enforcers. Many of them were from the Dominican order of monks. They arrested heretics. Then they put them on trial before a special religious court.

The Spanish Inquisition was founded in the late fifteenth century. At that time, King Ferdinand and Queen Isabella ruled Spain. The Spanish Inquisition sought out Catholic heretics. It also went after Muslims and Jews who had converted to Catholicism but were not sincere in their new faith. The punishments for heretics could be as mild as wearing special clothing. Or it could be as severe as being burned alive in a public square.

The Catholic Church ended the Spanish Inquisition in 1834. But enforcement of church policy continued under the Sacred Congregation of the Holy Office. Joseph Cardinal Ratzinger led this department of the Vatican for twenty-four years.

Ratzinger the task of outlining an important document on revelation, known in Latin as *Dei Verbum*, or *The Word of God*.

According to *Dei Verbum*, the Catholic Church "is a community that listens to and proclaims the word of God." This revelation comes in the form of the Holy

Trinity: the Father, the Son, and Holy Spirit. The Son appeared on Earth to reveal the existence of the Father and transmit the knowledge of God through the Holy Spirit. To understand revelation, the faithful must follow the priests and teachers of the church. If a person does not accept this authority, Catholicism becomes an endless argument. The result can be confusion and chaos and a loss of faith. On November 18, 1965, in the last days of Vatican II, *Dei Verbum* was approved. Father Ratzinger had taken part in one of the most important councils in church history. He felt optimistic about the future. He believed that the council had set the church on the right path.

Father Joseph Ratzinger in 1965

Catholics all over the world shared his opinion. In their eyes, the church had to change to keep up with the world outside the Vatican. The old medieval church no longer held the power to condemn and punish those who simply disagreed with its views. As an important example of this, the Vatican II council also ended the *Index Librorum Prohibitorum*, a list of books that Catholics were forbidden to read. The list included important authors such as Jonathan Swift, Daniel Defoe, Samuel Richardson, Laurence Stern, George Sand, Victor Hugo, Gustave Flaubert, John Milton, John Locke, Emile Zola, and Jean-Paul Sartre.

The Holy Office, which enforced the Index, remained open for business. It still had the important job of enforcing the rules of the church, setting down correct doctrine, punishing misbehavior of its members, and guiding theologians in their writings. It was the oldest office in the Vatican government and one of the most important. The prefect of the Holy Office held authority only slightly less than that of the pope himself.

Father Ratzinger returned to Germany and to teaching. Like many Catholic leaders, he believed in the guidance of Vatican II. The council had settled many difficult issues. Yet the most bitter debates were yet to come.

Tubingen is widely known as a city of learning. It is home to astronomers, poets, and philosophers. Joseph Ratzinger taught at Tubingen's school of theology in the 1960s.

Chapter **FOUR**

TROUBLED TIMES

IN **1966** **FATHER** **RATZINGER** **JOINED** **THE** **UNIVERSITY** of Tubingen, a world-famous school of theology in his native Bavaria. The teachers and the clergy of Germany respected his scholarship and the important role he had played at the Vatican Council.

But Father Ratzinger was also beginning the most difficult time of his life. The 1960s were confusing for Western society and for the church as well. Members of the church were challenging its traditional beliefs and rules. The ordination of women as priests, sexual practices, divorce, abortion, and contraception all became controversial topics. Many Catholics who disagreed with the official stand of the church on these issues were dropping out. Priests were experimenting with new ways of saying Mass and new ways of interpreting scripture. Many Catholics saw the pope in a new light. They saw him not as a leader but as an adviser. They thought they could accept or reject his instructions.

In many Catholic churches, priests were using new liturgies. This troubled Father Ratzinger. He believed that the traditional liturgies were sacred. To change them on a whim or to follow a modern style was to forget this very important fact. For Father Ratzinger, there could be no debate over divine revelation. It was as the church defined it. And no good Catholic should challenge this teaching.

TROUBLE AT THE UNIVERSITY

At Munster and Tubingen, Ratzinger took part in many debates over Catholic teaching. He also saw teachers and students abandoning traditional Catholicism and following radical political ideas. One of these was Marxism, the philosophy that gave rise to Communism. In this political system, a single party of elite members ruled. Private property was banned. And the state controlled industry, farming, trade, culture, religion, education—every aspect of people's lives.

Father Ratzinger saw Communism as the worst enemy of Christianity. Under a Communist regime, he believed, the people forgot the sacraments and ignored scripture. They replaced faith in God with faith in a political system. Such a system turned people into

Communist youths rally in the part of Berlin controlled by the Soviet Union. They carry a picture of Communist leader Joseph Stalin. Many Catholics saw Communism as a threat to their faith.

obedient workers and destroyed their spiritual life. They adopted an outlook on life in which working for the state was the supreme virtue.

Many teachers and students at Munster and Tubingen supported Communist beliefs. Some Catholic thinkers were encouraging rebellion against established institutions. Ratzinger saw it happening not just in poverty-stricken countries of Asia, Latin America, and Africa. Rebellion was also happening in his own country, where many young people felt shame at Germany's dark past. Catholic priests, to the horror of Father Ratzinger, were defying their superiors and the pope himself. In some countries, they were fostering revolution. They were speaking out for the overthrow of repressive governments and politicians.

Ratzinger debated these issues with his colleagues. He held firm against this new movement of "liberation theology." In this new movement, the church went beyond charity for the poor. It also helped them organize into a political force. That force fought for revolution against violent regimes, such as many of those in Central America. In his fight against liberation theology, Ratzinger often felt as if he were swimming against the tide. During his lectures, students often stood up to directly challenge his teaching. Several times, they demonstrated outside the lecture halls. They occupied seats within the halls and spoke out, preventing him from responding. Father Ratzinger was a quiet and shy person. He was used to the respect of his students, and he found it hard to deal with such defiance.

It seemed to Ratzinger that students were challenging the church's authority at every turn. The students wanted to forget church history. They wanted to bring politics directly into their religion. They demanded the right to select the chaplain of their parish—a right that traditionally belonged to the bishop. They wanted the church to become politically active, to speak out against what they saw as injustice. They also wanted the church to help overthrow tyrannical governments in foreign nations. The effort split the students and teachers. It forced them to join either the conservative side, which held to the traditions of the church, or the progressive side, which wanted the church to be politically active.

HUMANAE VITAE

The church had always instructed its members in their private lives. By tradition, Catholic families were often large. The church encouraged people to "be fruitful and multiply," in the words of the New Testament. The church banned the use of birth control. According to this teaching, preventing conception interfered with God's natural order of things.

In the 1960s, many Catholics believed the church should change its stand. They saw the use of birth control as a private decision and not the business of the church. In addition, scientists had invented a contraceptive pill. The pill made birth control easy and affordable.

Pope Paul VI, the successor to Pope John XXIII, resisted this new trend. The new pope wanted to return the church to its role as spiritual shepherd to the Catholic flock. He didn't want the church involved in politics or revolution. In personal matters, Paul wanted the church to provide the teaching he felt people wanted and needed. The matter of birth control was a perfect example. It involved hard decisions about the origin of life. In these matters, it was the duty of the Catholic Church to instruct on the church's traditional principle that all life is sacred—and not a matter where humans should interfere.

Pope Paul felt the need to make an official statement. On July 25, 1968, he responded with an encyclical, *Humanae Vitae, Encyclical of Pope Paul VI on the Regulation of Birth*. It stirred up even more controversy. The encyclical laid out the official position of the church. It called on couples to take their marriage seriously, to be responsible parents, and not to use any means of birth control:

> ... an act of mutual love which impairs the capacity to transmit life which God the Creator, through specific laws, has built into it, frustrates His design which constitutes the norm of marriage, and contradicts the will of the Author of life. Hence to use this divine gift while depriving it, even if only partially, of its meaning and purpose, is equally repugnant to the nature of man and of woman, and is consequently in opposition to the plan of God and His holy will.

Humanae Vitae banned the birth-control pill, the use of condoms, abortion, and any means of sterilization. According to the encyclical, such actions interfered with the will of God. If a couple wanted to prevent birth, they should practice abstinence. They could also use the rhythm method of birth control. With this method, a couple has sex only on days when the woman is in the infertile part of her monthly cycle and cannot conceive a child.

An uproar broke out immediately. The entire world seemed to react to *Humanae Vitae*. There were protests in newspapers, on television broadcasts, and in the streets. Many people pointed out the widespread poverty in the world, caused by overpopulation. How could the church pretend this was not a serious problem? Many priests and theologians also protested. The church seemed out of touch with the changing world. Living behind the high walls of the Vatican, the pope seemed to have ignored reality.

But the protest against *Humanae Vitae* was heard even within the walls of the Vatican. Many Catholics

A protester holds a sign in favor of birth control. Pope Paul's encyclical, Humanae Vitae, angered many Catholics and non-Catholics.

ignored the instruction. Others, including large numbers of priests and nuns, simply dropped out of the church. The pope felt surprise and dismay at the reaction. For the next ten years, he issued no more proclamations. He knew he would be remembered only for a document that began a bitter debate among Catholics, one that still continues.

MOVING TO REGENSBURG

Father Ratzinger wholeheartedly supported *Humanae Vitae*. For him and other church conservatives, the pope was taking a stand not just against birth control but also against the modern world. It seemed to Ratzinger that this changing world was making religion seem like an empty ceremony. It was leading

Father Ratzinger taught and studied at the University of Regensburg (above) *from 1968 to 1977.*

people to defy church teachings. As a result, they were losing respect for the pope and their sense of right and wrong.

In *Humanae Vitae*, Father Ratzinger heard the voice of church authority return in strength. In his mind, it was the duty of church leaders, especially the pope, to guide the Catholic flock—sternly, if necessary. The church offered this guidance on all matters, regardless of how private some might be. And it expected Catholics to follow it.

Still, Ratzinger had little appetite for debate and fighting. In late 1968, a new university in the Bavarian town of Regensburg invited him to join as a professor. Regensburg was just getting established, and Tubingen was one of the most important schools of theology in the world. Ratzinger found this an easy decision to make. At Regensburg, he believed, he could teach, study, and write in peace. In this small, quiet town on the Danube River, he hoped to escape political controversy and conflict. He could also live near his brother Georg, who was a choirmaster in the same city. He eagerly accepted.

Ratzinger eventually became dean and vice president at Regensburg. He built a house, where he lived with his sister. She served as his secretary. He settled down to the life he enjoyed, the life of a scholar and teacher. He had one more goal in life—to become a cardinal. He wanted to earn this highest reward for a life of service to the church.

Father Joseph Ratzinger in 1977

Chapter **FIVE**

DEFENDING
THE FAITH

JOSEPH RATZINGER'S WORK AT THE SECOND VATICAN
Council had brought him widespread respect within
the church. As a scholar and lecturer, Ratzinger had
often clashed with other theologians. But Pope Paul
VI supported him. And for Father Ratzinger that was
most important. Ratzinger followed the traditional
view that the pope was infallible. In other words, the
pope could make no errors in the matter of religious
teaching and guidance. He also believed that the
church should be ruled from the top down. In Father
Ratzinger's belief, accepted church doctrine should
never be challenged by contrary views, no matter
how popular such views were among scholars, students, or parishioners.

The church rewarded his opinion. In the spring of 1977, Ratzinger was appointed as the new archbishop of Munich and Freising. An archbishop is responsible for guiding the bishops of several provinces and cities. The episcopal see (district) of Munich and Freising is a large and important one in the heart of Catholic Germany. Just a few days after becoming archbishop, the pope named Archbishop Ratzinger a cardinal. The official ceremony, in which he accepted the cardinal's traditional red biretta (hat), took place on June 27. As a cardinal, Joseph Ratzinger belonged to the Sacred College. This group of men is responsible for meeting in Rome after the death of a pope and electing a new one. It is one of the most important responsibilities cardinals have.

THE NEW PAPACY

In August 1978, Pope Paul VI died. Cardinal Ratzinger traveled to Rome to take part in the conclave to select the new pope. He met the other members of the Sacred College. Many lived outside Europe and rarely traveled to Rome. On September 26, the Sacred College elected Albino Cardinal Luciani of the Italian city of Venice. This pope took the name of John Paul I, in honor of the previous two popes, John XXIII and Paul VI.

Soon after the conclave, Ratzinger traveled to Ecuador, a small country in South America. He had been invited to a Marian congress, an assembly of church members in honor of the Virgin Mary. While

Pope John Paul I died in 1978, shortly after becoming pope.

staying in the Ecuadorean capital city of Quito, he received the news that John Paul I had died after only a month in the papacy. Ratzinger and the other members of the Sacred College returned to Rome for another conclave. On October 22, 1978, they made a bold and surprising choice. They chose Karol Cardinal Wojtyla of Krakow, Poland. He was the first pope in 455 years who was not Italian. In honor of his predecessor, Wojtyla took the name of John Paul II.

Wojtyla was an outspoken critic of the Communist regime that ruled Poland. His selection represented a bold challenge to the Polish government and to other Communist regimes. All these regimes were opposed to the Catholic Church and all other churches. One of Wojtyla's first acts as pope was to pay a visit to his homeland. In June 1979, the Polish people turned out by the millions to greet the pope as a hero. They attended his masses and defied their government's ban on public assemblies. The pope's visit encouraged opposition to the regime. In the next year, workers at the shipyard in the Polish port of Gdansk openly challenged their leaders with a massive strike.

Ratzinger had met Wojtyla during the conclave that had elected John Paul I. He saw in this pope a strong defender of traditional Catholicism. Ratzinger enthusiastically supported Wojtyla's candidacy. In November 1980,

Pope John Paul II (left) and Cardinal Ratzinger during the pope's visit to Germany in November 1980

the pope honored Ratzinger with a visit to Germany. Cardinal Ratzinger hosted Wojtyla's stay in Munich.

John Paul II believed that the Vatican and the curia were in need of reform and of new men. He turned to Joseph Ratzinger in this effort. He believed Ratzinger could defend Catholicism from those who wanted to make the church into a political party and ignore its religious teachings. On November 25, 1981, the pope named Cardinal Ratzinger as prefect of the Congregation for the Doctrine of the Faith (CDF), the former Holy Office. In this position, Ratzinger corrected mistakes of members of the church in their writings and sermons. He guided Catholics on the right interpretation of scripture. He enforced church rules for its priests and bishops. And he punished those who defied the authority of the pope and the Vatican.

Ratzinger thought long and hard about his appointment to the CDF. He knew that he would have to postpone his true desire in life, to continue to study and write and serve his homeland as an archbishop. But for Cardinal Ratzinger, duty and service to the church was uppermost. He accepted the appointment.

PREFECT OF THE CDF

In the past, the Congregation for the Doctrine of the Faith had dealt with Protestants, with religious heretics, and with banned books. In the twentieth century, it was responsible for the purity of Catholic

THE CONGREGATION FOR THE DOCTRINE OF THE FAITH

The nine departments of the curia are known as congregations. The oldest of these is the Congregation for the Doctrine of the Faith. It was founded in 1542 by Pope Paul II to fight the many heresies of the time. The Protestant Reformation was spreading across northern Europe. In this movement, Christians openly defied the pope and the Catholic hierarchy. They saw the church as corrupt and incapable of ministering to the needs of the faithful. The wealth of the church, the sale of church offices, and the payments the church demanded for the forgiveness of sin angered Protestants.

The Protestant churches paid no attention to Catholic rules and doctrine. They had no priests or bishops. But in the eyes of the pope, this movement was heresy. It had to be stamped out. To defend the Catholic Church against this heresy, Pope Paul II organized the Sacred Congregation of the Universal Inquisition (later the Holy Office). In 1965 Pope Paul VI changed the name to the Congregation for the Doctrine of the Faith.

doctrine. It examined the writings and the public speaking of members of the church. Then it warned those whose ideas strayed too far from accepted tradition. It dealt with the church's inner problems. They included those who presented new and unacceptable theologies, those who committed acts of defiance against the pope and the Vatican, and those who committed immoral or illegal acts. Cardinal Ratzinger handled these problems on a daily basis and decided how to punish the guilty.

When Catholic priests openly disagreed with the church's positions on social issues, Ratzinger took action. One of these challengers was Father Charles Curran. He was a priest and a professor at the Catholic University of America in Washington, D.C. Curran believed that Catholics had the right to disagree with the church on social issues and make their own decisions about their private lives. He criticized *Humanae Vitae* and the church's doctrine about birth control. The CDF issued strong warnings to Curran. In 1986 Cardinal Ratzinger called Curran to Rome to meet with him. The two men could not agree on the issue of birth control or on many other issues. In 1987, when Curran still refused to follow the instructions of the CDF, the Vatican ordered that he be fired from his teaching post.

DEALING WITH LIBERATION THEOLOGY

As prefect of the CDF, Ratzinger faced many thorny issues. In his own view, the most dangerous for the church was still liberation theology. The idea of the church as a "liberator" of the poor—by supporting political movements and revolution—still caused debate within the church. Conservatives stood against liberation theology. Progressive and liberal members supported it. This time Cardinal Ratzinger had to enforce the church's official position on the idea. In his own opinion, only devotion to God brought true liberation. This meant freedom from sin and eternal life in heaven.

In the 1980s, Ratzinger handed down this stand with two important documents: *Libertatis Nuntius,* or On Liberation Theology, and *Libertatis Conscientia,* or On Freedom of Conscience. Both documents condemned liberation theology. The only liberation was through faith in God and the sacraments. But the church still had a role in helping the poor. The church offered charity, schools, and shelter to those who needed it. And the church could help support justice in all countries.

The pope stood firmly behind these pronouncements. At the same time, John Paul II was recognized as an

In 1989 West Germans watch East German border guards pull down the Berlin Wall that separated Communist Berlin from free Berlin.

enemy of the Communist regime, which had rigidly restricted the Catholic Church. In the 1980s, his firm stand led to action. The people of Poland staged strikes, demonstrations, and public meetings. In 1989 the Polish Communist regime fell from power. In the same year, the Berlin Wall, the massive barrier that separated democratic West Berlin from Communist East Germany, came down. All over the world, Communism was widely seen as a failure. The Soviet government also fell from power, and the Soviet Union broke up into fifteen independent republics. The Christian churches of Russia and Eastern Europe revived. They attracted parishioners without fear of any retaliation.

THE CHALLENGE OF MATERIALISM

Pope John Paul II had encouraged the revival of the Catholic Church in Eastern Europe. He was seen as an opponent of the Communist regimes. For this stand, many in his native country and around the world saw him as a hero. But the pope was looking for more than a change in government. He sought a spiritual revolution in Europe as well. He believed that the Catholic Church was losing ground. He believed the church should return to its history and tradition. He believed that it should affirm what it had taught for two thousand years. Priests and bishops should follow instructions from the Vatican and help the church to speak with a single voice. In this way, people could understand clearly what the church stood for. They would, once again, see the church as a central part of their lives.

Cardinal Ratzinger's job was to clarify this teaching and follow the pope's guidance. But for his efforts, Ratzinger came under constant criticism. Many critics saw him as too strict and conservative. In the United States, in particular, many American Catholics did not like Ratzinger's conservative theology.

But John Paul II supported Ratzinger without question. They met every week to discuss church controversies. The pope believed that Ratzinger's ideas about Christianity set an important example for the priests and bishops of the church. They were the church leaders who had direct contact with the world's Catholics. Ratzinger believed in the mysteries of Catholicism. The mysteries included the virgin birth of Christ, his ascension (rise) into heaven, and the presence of Christ in the bread and wine of the Catholic Mass. The pope also believed in these ancient mysteries. He saw them as the foundation of everything the church did—daily Mass, missionary work, charity, and education. In this view, everything the church taught was based on the life of Christ and the mysteries surrounding his death and resurrection.

Despite the fall of Communism, John Paul II still felt dismay at the state of the church. In the former Communist world, people seemed to take a stronger interest in business, money, and possessions than in their faith. This was easy to understand in countries where poverty had been widespread. But people around the world—even in Europe and the United States—were also defying the pope's teachings. People disagreed with him on divorce and birth control. They ignored Mass. And many lost interest in theology and the priesthood.

This materialism challenged John Paul II's interest in the life of the mind. It challenged his belief in the moral and spiritual side of human beings. Europe and the United States seemed to have lost this spiritual outlook in the quest for goods, money, and comfort. But other parts of the world held out the promise of a spiritual revival. In Latin America, Africa, and Asia, the church was gaining converts. The pope, who often traveled to these parts of the world, was winning a following. John Paul II and many other church officials saw the possibility of a Catholic revival in lands far from the church's headquarters in Rome.

Pope John Paul II greets the faithful from his popemobile in Hungary in 1991. His traveling decreased as he became frail and sick.

Chapter SIX

CARDINAL RATZINGER'S BATTLES

THROUGH THE **1990**S, CARDINAL RATZINGER'S WORK as prefect of the CDF remained demanding and difficult. He felt loyalty to the pope and devotion to his job, but he was growing old. He thought about retiring and following a simple dream. He wanted to return to his life as a scholar in Germany. But the pope did not want to see Cardinal Ratzinger leave the Vatican. He believed Ratzinger was his most important ally for his views on the church and its mission. John Paul II also set an inspiring example by his own courage in the face of old age, frailty, and illness. Cardinal Ratzinger stayed on at the Vatican. He tended to the failing health of the pope and prepared for another sacred conclave.

FIGHTING RELATIVISM

Ratzinger kept up the fight for church doctrine. In 2000 the CDF issued *Dominus Iesus, Declaration on Universality*. In this document, the CDF gave the Vatican's stand on the world's other faiths. It stated there were certain "indispensible elements of Christian doctrine" that no Catholic could deny. The document spelled out the eternal truth of this doctrine. There could be no salvation except through the church and its sacraments. In no uncertain terms, it condemned the modern trend to "relativism."

In Ratzinger's view, relativism replaced Marxism as the most serious threat to the church. Relativism means that all faiths are valid. It considers Jesus just one of many inspired teachers and healers. And relativism holds that Christians should respect the beliefs of those outside their church as equal to their own. Relativism also means that the Catholic Church must be flexible in applying its rules and doctrines in non-Western societies. The goal of relativism is harmony among all religions.

In Ratzinger's view, however, relativism is not valid. The Catholic Church offers the only true doctrine. There is only one redeemer for all humankind, Jesus Christ. And the only way to heaven is through the Catholic Church and its sacraments. This holds true for everyone, not just those born and raised in Christian nations. It is the mission of the church to spread the word of this truth to the entire world. In an interview, Ratzinger expressed his view clearly:

> Christ is totally different from all the founders of other religions, and he cannot be reduced to a Buddha, a Socrates or a Confucius. He is really the bridge between heaven and earth, the light of truth who has appeared to us. . . . I would say that at the present time the dialogue with the other religions is the most important point: to understand how, on one hand, Christ is unique, and on the other, how he answers all others, who are precursors of [came before] Christ, and who are in dialogue with Christ.

A statue of Buddha (left) *in a temple in Myanmar. Buddhists recognize Buddha as their god. Joseph Ratzinger views relativism (treating all faiths as equal) as the most serious threat to the Catholic Church.*

Joseph Cardinal Ratzinger celebrates Mass in Rome on June 22, 2000, during his time as prefect of the CDF.

For Cardinal Ratzinger, only one truth exists. The church must defend it, even if it means losing members who disagree. According to Ratzinger, there is nothing relative about the truth. Those who believe that this truth is different for different people or that it has various shades of meaning are making a serious mistake. This mistake allows some to twist the truth for selfish or evil purposes. It allows them to put themselves above the church and the pope himself.

Ratzinger had seen it for himself in Nazi Germany. Pope John Paul II had lived through the same situation in Communist Poland. These regimes had proclaimed that the people should obey the leaders of the state and not the church. When they closed the churches and banned Mass, the people had lost the guidance of faith.

DIFFICULT ISSUES

Many Catholics criticized Ratzinger's views and his work as prefect of the CDF. They pointed out that, in its investigations, the CDF was violating basic civil rights of citizens in many countries. It violated the right to know one's accuser, the right to know the charges brought against a person, and the right to an open, public trial. They saw Ratzinger as an inflexible authority who could not be questioned. Nearly every statement dealing with Catholic doctrines had to be approved by a single man—Cardinal Ratzinger. He had the power to excommunicate (expel from the church) any person who disagreed with his view. To many people, this made him too powerful.

These critics believed that Catholicism had to change. They thought the church should accept a variety of religions and philosophies. It should stop trying to convert non-Catholics, stop directing the private lives of families, and accept the role of a worldwide charity. If it did not, then the church would become irrelevant. It would become a thing of the past.

Catholics would drop away, stop attending Mass, stop paying attention to the pope and the Vatican, and eventually lose their faith altogether.

Critics thought some big changes should be made. For example, they thought that the church should change its stand on birth control. Many Catholics thought the decision to have a baby is a private one. They felt the decision is based on factors that were no longer the church's business. The church's stand on homosexuality was also challenged. In Ratzinger's view, gay men and lesbian women are fully spiritual human beings created by God. They can attend Mass and receive Holy Communion. They can ask for redemption of their sins and achieve salvation. But in his view, they are committing a sin if they are not celibate. He believes the Bible condemns homosexuality and so must the church. Among several other passages in the Bible, he quotes Leviticus, a book of the Old Testament. The passage states: "If there is a man who lies with a male as those who lie with a woman, both of them have committed a detestable act; they shall surely be put to death. Their blood guiltness is upon them." (Leviticus 20:13)

In Ratzinger's view, the traditional family—one man and one woman and their offspring—is the only proper arrangement of family life. Ratzinger believes that the church should strive to make homosexuals see the error of their ways. Further, the church should not permit homosexuals to be ordained as priests.

A man holding a crucifix (center) *protests against gay marriage as two men protest in support of gay marriage* (right). *As prefect of the CDF, Cardinal Ratzinger stood against gay marriage and the ordination of gays as priests.*

The church could no longer punish people who disagree with it by turning them over to authorities for imprisonment or execution. But the church could warn or excommunicate members. Ratzinger stood firm on these issues. He answered all those who opposed church policy. Pope John Paul II let it be known that he agreed with all of these stands. In his writings and speeches, the pope also spoke against the dangers of relativism. He felt the philosophy did not point out the truth of the Catholic doctrine and the error of all others.

A RULE OF SILENCE

As prefect of the CDF, the toughest issue Cardinal Ratzinger faced was a scandal in the late 1990s involving some Catholic priests. In the United States, Europe, and Latin America, adult men were claiming that when they were younger, they had suffered sexual abuse from priests. The men claimed the abuse had happened during the years they attended Catholic schools or served as altar boys, who assist priests during Catholic services. The accusations gained publicity in newspapers and on television. In some cases, the accusations led to court trials. In others, the church quietly settled the cases with the accusers. It paid them money as reparation.

Many people disagreed with the way the Catholic Church handled the sexual abuse scandal in the United States. Cardinal Ratzinger's rule of silence did not stop Catholics from protesting (right).

In the eyes of many, the accusations and trials were damaging the reputation of the church. Cardinal Ratzinger was responsible for dealing with this issue. He wanted the church—rather than the police or the justice system—to handle the issue. He also enforced a tough rule of silence. In 1962 Pope John XXIII had set down the rule in *Crimine Solicitationies,* or "Instruction on Proceeding in Cases of Solicitation." The rule had dealt only with abuse when priests heard confessions from members of their congregations. It stated that anyone involved in such a case had to keep silent. The case must not be discussed with anyone, especially not with the press. Such cases had to be handled within the church. If anyone broke the rule of silence, he would be subject to excommunication.

Cardinal Ratzinger applied the rule to all accusations of abuse, not just those that took place in confession. In May 2001, he sent a letter to the bishops of the church, stating that the *Crimine Solicitationies* law was still in effect. He also claimed that the church had the authority to judge any case where the accuser had reached eighteen, the legal age of adulthood in most countries. Ratzinger insisted that the cases come to the CDF. The CDF could then send the case to a local church court. There, the judge and the lawyers are priests. Ratzinger believed the church had the right to investigate these cases and hold tribunals in secret. He also wanted the church to keep all evidence hidden from the public for ten years.

This rule meant that priests and all others within the church hierarchy could not bring any cases to the police or to the public through writings or statements. Some outsiders saw Cardinal Ratzinger's instruction as a cover-up. But he defended it by claiming that sexual abuse by priests was not a widespread problem. He believed it to be a media creation, played up by the press to gain an audience. He believed that such cases were no more common within the church than in the secular, or nonreligious, world.

Some claimed that the vow of celibacy—the priest's traditional vow to abstain from sex and from marriage—was to blame for the problem. Cardinal Ratzinger and all other Vatican officials strongly defended this traditional vow. In the Catholic doctrine, a priest of the church must model himself after Jesus Christ. He must remain unmarried and childless. He must turn his attention and devotion to a higher cause. In effect, he is married to the church.

The sexual abuse scandal was very damaging to the Catholic Church. The church could not keep the cases from becoming public. Many people lost their faith in the church, and it paid millions of dollars to settle the cases. Cardinal Ratzinger's firm rule of secrecy may have helped the church keep the scandal from growing even worse. But for some, it also gave the impression that the Vatican had much to hide and did not care about the victims.

DEFYING THE BAN

Cardinal Ratzinger also dealt firmly with a challenge to the church rule against ordaining women as priests. In June 2002, Romulo Antonio Braschi, a priest from Argentina, had ordained seven women as priests. He held the ceremony on a boat in the middle of the Danube River in Germany. Braschi was a leader of the Schismatic Catholic Apostolic Church of Brazil, a group that had split from the mother church in 1945.

The ordination of the seven women was a direct challenge to Cardinal Ratzinger. His hometown lay just a few miles from the site of Braschi's ceremony. On July 10, Ratzinger gave the group twelve days to give up their action and ask forgiveness. If they refused, they would be excommunicated from the church. In his declaration, Ratzinger stated:

> The . . . 'priestly ordination' constitutes the simu-
> lation of a sacrament [is like performing a sacra-
> ment] and is thus invalid and null, as well as
> constituting a grave offense to the divine consti-
> tution of the Church [breaking the laws of the
> church]. Such an action is an affront to the dig-
> nity of women, whose specific role in the Church
> and society is distinctive and irreplaceable.

Braschi and the seven women he had ordained did not back down. On August 5, Ratzinger carried out his threat of excommunication. The declaration officially broke all ties between the Catholic Church and Braschi and the ordained women. It called on them to repent their actions and return to the church.

Cardinal Ratzinger, with the support of Pope John Paul II, had issued several opinions and pronouncements on the subject of ordaining women. These opinions would not consider a change in the age-old rule preventing women from becoming priests. The role of women is to help in parish and missionary work, to aid the poor and sick, and to work as teachers. In the official words of the CDF and the pope, this was an "infallible" teaching that could not be questioned or debated. They claimed the authority of biblical teaching and church tradition.

The sexual abuse scandal and the debate over the ordination of women cast a shadow over the church. At the same time, however, Pope John Paul II was winning support for his courage and energy. His travels to every corner of the globe drew huge crowds. He won praise from Catholics and non-Catholics. With Cardinal Ratzinger at his side, the Polish pope had put up a strong defense of Catholic traditions. Pope John Paul II believed Cardinal Ratzinger was the one to carry on this role.

A CLASH OF RELIGION AND POLITICS

Normally, Catholic leaders, including Joseph Ratzinger, prefer to stay out of election politics. They avoid taking sides in support of one candidate or another. But as prefect of the Congregation for the Doctrine of the Faith, Cardinal Ratzinger believed that on certain important social issues, the church had to speak out. During the U.S. presidential election of 2004, Democratic candidate John Kerry publicly stated that he supported the right to legal abortion.

Democratic presidential candidates including John Kerry (far left) attend a pro-choice banquet in 2002. Cardinal Ratzinger, as prefect of the CDF, declared that John Kerry, a Catholic, should be denied Holy Communion because of his pro-choice stance on abortion.

As a Catholic, Kerry was challenging the church's teaching on this issue. The church holds that abortion is immoral and a grave sin under any circumstances. Because of Kerry's position on abortion, Cardinal Ratzinger and the Vatican declared that he should be denied Holy Communion at the Catholic Mass. But, many church leaders don't agree. Kerry attended Mass at the Paulist Center, a more liberal group of Catholic worshippers in Boston, Massachusetts. There, he received Holy Communion.

Pope John Paul II greets Catholic followers in Dakar, Senegal, a country in West Africa.

Chapter **SEVEN**

THE CONCLAVE OF THE SACRED COLLEGE

POPE JOHN PAUL II'S DEATH IN **2005** POSED A great challenge to the Catholic Church. The choice of a successor to John Paul II would be difficult. He had been one of the most popular religious leaders in history. He had been pope for twenty-six years, one of the longest reigns in church history. He had made 104 trips all over the world. He had traveled to Asia, Africa, the Middle East, South America, Europe, and North America. His visits to Poland and his declarations against the Communist regime there had helped Poles to overcome an oppressive government. Many devout Catholics supported his firm stand on important social issues. Others disagreed with these opinions. Still, they admired John Paul II's unshakeable faith and charisma.

After Pope John Paul II's funeral, 117 cardinals assembled for the conclave. They would have to discuss the future of the church and find the best man to lead it. That man would become the 265th pope of the Catholic Church. The cardinals met in secret, behind closed and locked doors. They were forbidden to meet privately among themselves or speak to the media about their debate. The announcement would be made in the traditional way. A fire would be lit in the fireplace of the Sistine Chapel, which would serve as the meeting hall. If no pope had been elected, dry straw would be burned, creating black smoke. If the cardinals decided on a new pope, officials would burn moist straw. The whitened smoke would be the signal that meant *habemus papem,* or "we have a pope."

The cardinals had many issues to consider. In Europe, the historic home of the church, Catholicism was declining. Many people saw the church as a relic of history. Many ignored its teachings on marriage and divorce, on family planning and birth control. They disagreed with the church on the proper response to serious poverty and injustice. Many saw its ban on female priests and its strict condemnation of abortion, euthanasia, and homosexuality as out of step with the reality of the modern world.

The cardinals had to consider the background of the new pope. What part of the world would he come from? Would it be best to choose another pope from Europe to try to revive the church's strength there? Or would it be better to reach out to Africa or Latin America? For example, Cardinal Arinze of Nigeria was one of the church's most popular leaders. Jorge Mario Cardinal Bergoglio of Argentina was widely respected by the cardinals and in his home country. And he often spoke of the need to help the poor.

Should the new pope be a pastoral leader, who traveled widely and worked to bring people into the Catholic community? Or should he be a scholar, who had lived a life of study and prayer? Should he be someone who had written important books and articles on the faith? Should he be an official of the Vatican, who knew best how to lead the church and had the respect of the other cardinals? Or should he be a complete outsider? What should his stand be on the many debates within the church on social issues?

THE BALLOTING

In the Sistine Chapel, a chamberlain and his staff handed out several paper ballots to the cardinals. To handle the voting, the conclave then selected nine officials. It needed three scrutineers to count the votes and three revisers to check the count of the scrutineers. It also needed three *infirmarii*. The infirmarii handled votes from those cardinals who, because of illness, could not be in the chapel itself. The infirmarii would leave the chapel, collect the votes from the sick and elderly cardinals, and return as quickly as possible. Then those ballots would be counted.

For each vote, the cardinals wrote their selection on small rectangular ballots. The cardinals were supposed to disguise their handwriting as much as possible. They also had to write out the name of their

The voting of the sacred conclave takes place in the Sistine Chapel, which is famous for its ceiling and the wall behind the altar (above) painted by the sixteenth-century artist Michelangelo.

candidate in full. Initials or partial names made the ballots invalid. They folded the papers and then held them in the air. When all were finished writing, the cardinals walked to the chapel altar one at a time. They swore an oath that they had followed the rules. Then they dropped the ballots into a large silver chalice. The scrutineers collected ballots from cardinals too weak or ill to walk to the altar, while the infirmarii brought in the ballots from the cardinals outside the chapel. This system of voting, in full view of the cardinals and election officials, makes it almost impossible for anyone to cheat in a papal election.

After the ballots are collected, one scrutineer shakes the chalice to mix the ballots. A second scrutineer counts them. If the number of ballots does not match the number of cardinals voting, the ballots are burned. Then another vote is taken. Any ballot with more than one name, as well as ballots with nothing written on them, are thrown out. If the scrutineers discover one ballot folded inside another, they examine the names written on them. If the two names are the same, they count a single vote. If the names are different, the ballots are thrown out.

If the number of valid ballots is correct, they are read out aloud, one by one. A scrutineer writes down the count for each candidate. A candidate must win at least two-thirds of the vote to be declared a winner. In that case, the revisers double-check the number of ballots and the tallies. After each round of voting, the ballots are burned. Burning the ballots in plain view of everyone assures that they can't be hidden from sight and used again. In addition, for each round of voting, new scrutineers, revisers, and informarii are chosen at random. This makes it nearly impossible for a group of cardinals to secretly plot to elect any one candidate.

KEEPING SECRETS

During and after the funeral ceremonies for Pope John Paul II, many of the cardinals had given interviews to reporters. They talked openly about the state of the church and how it should be guided in the future. Some gave their opinion about good candidates for the papacy—the men known as *papabili*. In many conversations, the name of Cardinal Ratzinger came up. But the Vatican has an old saying: "Those who enter the conclave as a pope, leave as a cardinal." In other words, men expecting to be elected pope are often disappointed.

A strict rule of silence began after the conclave of the Sacred College began. Throughout the election, the cardinals had to keep quiet about the proceedings. They were forbidden to meet among themselves, in public or in private, to promote one candidate over another. They could not form parties for any candidates. Nor could they make agreements with anyone about how they would vote. They left at the end of each day to return to the Hotel Santa Marta, within the Vatican. They stayed in private

Jorge Mario Bergoglio (right), cardinal of *Argentina, had many supporters who wanted him to be the next pope.*

rooms for the night. The doors of the hotel were closed to all outsiders. And the cardinals were not permitted to leave for any reason or even look out of their windows. The windows were sealed shut with drawn blinds.

In the first round of voting on April 18, the cardinals voted for more than thirty candidates. Cardinal Ratzinger headed the list with forty-seven votes. Jorge Mario Cardinal Bergoglio of Argentina won ten. The first round of papal elections often went this way. No winner was selected. The cardinals just showed their support for a variety of trusted friends, associates, and mentors who had no realistic chance of winning.

In the second round, Ratzinger increased his lead and emerged as a clear favorite. He won sixty-five votes to Bergoglio's thirty-five. In the third vote, Ratzinger won seven additional votes. This brought his total to seventy-two. Yet Bergoglio collected forty. That amount would prevent Ratzinger from gaining the two-thirds majority he needed to win.

Supporters of Cardinal Bergoglio were making a very strong statement about their desire for a pope from Latin America. It was a region that had grown more important to the Catholic Church during the

Joseph Ratzinger speaks to the crowd in Saint Peter's Square shortly after being elected pope in 2005. He took the name Benedict XVI.

papacy of John Paul II. But they also wanted to avoid a stalled election. And they had to consider the view of Cardinal Bergoglio. In his words and actions, the cardinal from Argentina made it clear that he did not want to be the next leader of the Catholic Church.

The fourth round of voting took place on April 19. Cardinal Ratzinger overcame the challenge from Cardinal Bergoglio and won eighty-four votes. That was a few more than the two-thirds needed. As millions of people around the world watched from Vatican Square and on television, white smoke emerged from the Sistine Chapel chimney. Jorge Cardinal Estevez of the South American nation of Chile stepped out on a balcony and announced "Habemus Papem!" The crowd cheered. The crowd marveled at the historic spectacle of another successful conclave, a tradition that goes back so many centuries. The crowd looked carefully into the room behind the window. A white-haired man was coming into view. Cardinal Estevez stepped aside, and Joseph Cardinal Ratzinger followed him onto the balcony as the new pope, Benedict XVI.

In his speeches and actions, Cardinal Ratzinger had shown that he would uphold the tradition of the church against any and all new beliefs and radical innovations. He would put Catholicism on its right, traditional path. And he would keep to the business of salvation, of charitable service to the poor, and of bringing the Bible and the word of God to nonbelievers.

This, in his opinion, was the sincere desire of Pope John Paul II, one of the most popular and influential popes in history.

WHY CARDINAL RATZINGER?

Many people had predicted the election of Joseph Ratzinger as the new pope. He had spent more than twenty years in the Vatican. And he led the most important office in the church. He had been a well-known and respected writer and teacher since the 1960s. And he had earned the close friendship of John Paul II, although his life had been very different. While the Polish pope had been an active traveler, Ratzinger was a homebody, a man who lived to study and pray. John Paul II was an activist, constantly seeking to improve the church. Ratzinger was a true conservative. He held to tradition, respected authority, and preferred not to make waves. John Paul II's populism reached out to Catholics and non-Catholics alike. Ratzinger's reserve tended to keep those who didn't follow his faith or who disagreed with his views at arm's length.

It may have been this conservative style the cardinals most appreciated during their conclave. John Paul II had been like a religious rock star, making waves wherever he went. He had taken an active part in world affairs. He had spoken out on issues such as war, poverty, Communism, and religious freedom. The cardinals were now seeking a man of reserve. They wanted peace and quiet in the church. Author Greg Tobin, describing the scene just after the election of Benedict XVI, writes:

> The crowd on Saint Peter's Square on Tuesday evening already noted his reserve and perhaps sensed that something was missing—Benedict XVI is not a populist [a man of the people]! But is it possible that the cardinals not only accepted these "deficits" in comparison to John Paul II as something they just had to put up with. It is in fact possible that they deliberately sought such qualities. After a turbulent pontificate [restless term of office], more calm was needed.

Nevertheless, the chances of Benedict XVI experiencing a calm, reserved, and peaceful reign over the Catholic Church are not high. Many vigorously disagree with his conservative position on issues such as the ordination of women and married men, liberation theology, and homosexuality. Many Catholics ignore the instruction against birth control. The strict discipline he exercised in the Congregation for the Doctrine of the Faith stirs up anger and resentment. The new pope faces challenges that will demand his close attention, energy, and conviction.

Joseph Cardinal Ratzinger became the 265th pope of the Roman Catholic Church in April 2005.

Chapter **EIGHT**

CHALLENGES OF THE FUTURE

POPE BENEDICT **XVI** NOW HOLDS ONE OF THE MOST powerful offices on earth. His word is law to many Catholics around the world. His opinion matters on many vital issues. He upholds a tradition stretching back more than two thousand years, while also leading the Catholic Church into a new millennium. How will he lead, and what example will he set? In the first months after he became pope, everyone wanted to know.

Modern times and events have powerful effects on Catholicism. The pope speaks out on spiritual matters to about one billion Catholics. But he also offers guidance on how they should live—publicly and privately. Every important social issue that concerns Catholics also concerns the pope. Catholics expect him to give his views according to church law and tradition and guide them according to his vision of the future. The pope is often called the keeper of the Catholic flock. That is why fans of Pope Benedict often call him their "German shepherd."

THE GLOBAL CATHOLIC CHURCH

An important challenge for Pope Benedict XVI will be keeping the church together. Pope John Paul II made 104 trips—more than all other popes combined—to every continent on earth (except Antarctica). His presence in so many places helped people see the human side of the distant Vatican. It also made the church a strong presence for those who lived far from Rome. Through most of his papacy, he was an energetic and vigorous man who enjoyed the challenge of constant travel. Pope Benedict XVI has spent most of his life indoors, in his study, reading, writing, and making decisions as prefect of the Congregation for the Doctrine of the Faith. Many question whether he, who was seventy-eight when he became pope, will show the same energy as John Paul II.

Another challenge to the church involves geography. In the late twentieth century, the focus of Catholicism moved to the Southern Hemisphere. The largest population of practicing Catholics lives in Latin America. There, poverty and injustice remain burning issues, causing angry debate and, in some places, violent conflict. In Africa the church competes with other faiths, in particular Islam, for the loyalty of the people. Much of Africa also faces extreme poverty and widespread disease, such as AIDS and malaria. And the church's ban on the use of all birth control—including condoms—exposes many people to AIDS.

Islam and Christianity have been in conflict for centuries. This has been true ever since the early spread of the Islamic faith in the Near East, North Africa, and southern Europe in the early Middle Ages (A.D. 600 to 750). Both Islam and Christianity claim to be true faiths. They must be accepted by their believers to the exclusion of all others. Many people of Islamic countries see Christian churches, such as the Catholic Church, as symbols of colonialism. In the past, European nations had colonized (occupied) their lands. Catholic missionaries (religious teachers) had tried to convert the people to a new religion. In some places, this led to the persecution of non-Catholics.

Catholics sometimes point to Muslims who practice violence. They point out terrorist attacks in the early twenty-first century that targeted Christians and were carried out in the name of Islam. Some accuse Muslims of wanting to destroy Western civilization and establish a new Islamic empire. In this view, political goals are based on religious ideas that turn into crusades. In a crusade, fighters see themselves as committing violence for a sacred cause.

RELEVANCE IN THE TWENTY-FIRST CENTURY

The church is struggling to remain relevant (meaningful) in many areas of the world, particularly Europe and the United States. In these wealthy regions, many people have forgotten or never received religious teaching. They may not know the lessons of the Bible, the words of the Mass, and the sacraments of baptism and communion. Secular society has replaced the church with the pursuit of wealth and leisure time. John T. McGreevy, a professor at Notre Dame, one of the most influential Catholic universities in the United States, describes the changing attitudes:

> The percentage of Catholic schoolchildren enrolled in Catholic schools is steadily declining, and after-school programs in religious education remain badly underdeveloped. At Notre Dame, where I teach and where almost all of my students are Catholic, professors in entry-level classes cannot assume basic knowledge of the Bible, the sacraments, or Church history.

The election of Ratzinger as pope may have been meant to directly address the decline of the Catholic Church in the West. Ratzinger is viewed by many as a fundamentalist, a strict conservative on doctrine and theology. In his own view, his loyalty to Catholic tradition helps the church defend itself against the secular world. He believes secularism threatens to completely overcome the Christian faith. Taking a stand on abortion, homosexuality, birth control, and euthanasia means the church still stands for values taught in the Bible. In Ratzinger's view, this is the church's mission.

WOMEN IN THE CHURCH

When John Paul II was pope, people within and outside the church called for women to play a more powerful, official role in the church. The rule keeping women out of the priesthood has been followed for

Some religions have women priests, such as the Right Reverend Ann Tottenham (above) of the Episcopal Church. The Roman Catholic Church, led by Pope Benedict XVI, does not believe women should be priests. Many Catholics hope that will change.

two thousand years. In 1994 Pope John Paul II wrote a letter titled *Ordinatio Sacerdotalis* (On Reserving Priestly Ordination to Men Alone). It stated that the church had no authority to ordain women and that this opinion was rooted in the teaching of the Bible. Nevertheless, many saw this tradition as outdated. They believe this discrimination against women is against the secular laws of many countries. They feel it puts the church out of step with modern societies.

Many people point out the declining number of young men entering Catholic seminaries. As a result, the church has fewer ordained priests. Fewer men, it seems, are willing to commit themselves to lifelong celibacy. The answer, in the view of some people, is to allow priests to marry and women to become priests as well. But Pope Benedict XVI sees the ordination of women as defiance of the Vatican and of church tradition. In the eyes of those who support women in the priesthood, however, his opinion threatens to weaken the church further. In this view, many will continue to see the church as irrelevant and out of touch with modern reality.

The most important challenge to the church, in Ratzinger's own view, is to protect human life from the moment of conception to the moment of death. He will lead the church to fight against abortion, euthanasia, and the death penalty. Under Benedict XVI's guidance, the church will also speak out against the cloning of animals or human beings—creating life from a copy of genetic material created in a laboratory. In the pope's view, such actions allow humans to replace the will of God with their own desires. These actions allow people to disrupt the natural order of things, which offers humankind eternal life and redemption from sin. Science cannot care for the soul, which is the role of the church. The pope worries that faith in science leads people away from the church's teaching. He fears that people will lose their vital spirituality.

Dolly the Sheep (below) *made the issue of cloning real for many people. In 1996 Dolly became the first mammal to be cloned.*

In his writings, the new pope cited this Bible verse from the book of 2 Timothy as the essence of his belief. This is the standard he will uphold:

> Preach the word, be urgent in season and out of season, convince, rebuke and exhort, be unfailing in patience and in teaching. For the time is coming when people will not endure sound teaching, but having itching ears they will accumulate for themselves teachers to suit their own likings, and will turn away from listening to the truth and wander into myths. As for you, always be steady, endure suffering, do the work of an evangelist, fulfill your ministry.
>
> Saint Paul, 2 Tim. 4:2–5

Pope Benedict XVI sees his role as guiding a huge flock of Catholic believers, protecting them from false ideas, and showing them what he believes is the true wisdom of the church fathers. He works in the shadow of the popular John Paul II, who in the eyes of many was a saint and one of the greatest popes in history. Benedict XVI wants only to fill the role he knows best: teacher and counselor in the Catholic faith.

On January 25, 2006, Pope Benedict released the first encyclical of his papacy. He called this lesson *Deus Caritas Est*, or "God Is Love." In this message, the pope states that the love of others makes a person stronger. Commitment and marriage, and not just

Pope Benedict XVI addresses the 2005 World Youth Jamboree in Germany. There are more than one billion Catholics in the world.

gratifying sexual desire, are the ultimate purpose of love. Charity toward others is the church's expression of that love. It is as important as the liturgy or the beliefs of the church.

In part of the encyclical, Pope Benedict XVI summed up his view of faith and love: "In a world where the name of God is sometimes associated with vengeance or even a duty of hatred and violence, this message is both timely and significant. For this reason, I wish in my first Encyclical to speak of the love which God lavishes upon us and which we in turn must share with others."

TIMELINE

1927 On April 16, Joseph Alois Ratzinger is born in Marktl am Inn, Germany.

1929 The Ratzinger family moves to Tittmoning.

1932 The Ratzingers move to Aschau am Inn.

1937 Joseph Ratzinger's father retires and moves to Hufschlag, near Traunstein. Joseph attends the gymnasium (secondary school) of Traunstein.

1939 Germany invades Poland, and World War II breaks out in Europe.

1941 As required by law, Joseph Ratzinger joins the Hitler Youth.

1943 Ratzinger is drafted into an antiaircraft unit. He is put to work building defenses against Allied air raids.

1944 Ratzinger builds antitank traps and other defenses to prepare for a Soviet invasion of Austria.

1945 At the close of World War II in Europe, Ratzinger is held briefly in an American prisoner-of-war camp. He enters Saint Michael's Seminary in the town of Traunstein.

1947 Ratzinger begins attending the University of Munich, where he studies philosophy and theology.

1951 He and his brother Georg are ordained as priests into the Catholic Church.

1953 Joseph Ratzinger wins his doctorate in theology with a thesis on Saint Augustine.

1957 A treatise on Saint Bonaventure wins Ratzinger the habilitation, an academic honor that allows him to work as a full professor of theology.

1958 Father Ratzinger becomes a professor of theology at Freising Superior School of Philosophy and Theology.

1959 Ratzinger joins the theological faculty at the University of Bonn.

1963 Ratzinger accepts a post at the University of Munster. During the Second Vatican Council, which lasts from 1962 until 1965, he serves as a consultant to Joseph Cardinal Frings.

1966 Ratzinger is appointed professor of dogmatic theology at the University of Tubingen.

1969 Unhappy with the religious debates and radical teaching at Tubingen, Ratzinger moves to the University of Regensburg.

1977 In March Father Ratzinger is appointed archbishop of Munich and Freising. Shortly afterward, on June 27, Pope Paul VI appoints him as a cardinal of the church.

1980 Cardinal Ratzinger hosts a visit by Pope John Paul II to Germany.

1981 Pope John Paul II names Cardinal Ratzinger as the prefect (head) of the Congregation for the Doctrine of the Faith.

1986 Cardinal Ratzinger begins work on a new catechism of the Catholic Church.
1991 Cardinal Ratzinger completes the new catechism.
2002 Cardinal Ratzinger is named dean of the College of Cardinals.
2005 A papal conclave elects Cardinal Ratzinger as the new pope after the death of John Paul II. Ratzinger takes the name Benedict XVI.
2006 Pope Benedict XVI issues his first encyclical, *Deus Caritas Est*, "God Is Love."

SOURCE NOTES

52 Paul VI, *Humanae Vitae: Encyclical of Pope Paul VI on the Regulation of Birth*, Vatican, July 25, 1968, http://www.vatican.va/holy_father/paul_vi/encyclicals/documents/hf_p-vi_enc_25071968_humanae-vitae_en.html. (September 28, 2005).

71 Matthew E. Bunson, *We Have a Pope! Benedict XVI* (Huntington, IN: Our Sunday Visitor Publishing, 2005), 191.

79 "Declaration on Priestly Ordination of Catholic Women," *Our Lady's Warriors*, July 10, 2002, http://www.ourladyswarriors.org/dissent/cdfpriestess.htm. (October 4, 2005).

93 Greg Tobin, *Holy Father, Benedict XVI, Pontiff for a New Era*, (New York: Sterling Publishing, 2005), 111.

98 John T. McGreevy, "Central America: After Pope John Paul II," *New Republic*, April 18, 2005, 20.

BIBLIOGRAPHY

Allen, John, Jr. *Pope Benedict XVI: A Biography of Joseph Ratzinger*. New York: Continuum, 2005.
Bunson, Matthew E. *We Have a Pope! Benedict XVI*. Huntington, IN: Our Sunday Visitor Publishing, 2005.

Fischer, H. J. *Pope Benedict XVI: A Personal Portrait*. New York: Crossroad Publishing Company, 2005.

John Paul II. *Memory and Identity: Conversations at the Dawn of a Millennium*. New York: Rizzoli, 2005.

Lo Bello, Nino. *The Incredible Book of Vatican Facts and Papal Curiosities: A Treasury of Trivia*. Liguori, MO: Liguori Publications, 1998.

Pham, John Peter. *Heirs of the Fisherman: Behind the Scenes of Papal Death and Succession*. New York: Oxford University Press, 2004.

Ratzinger, Joseph. *Milestones: Memoirs 1927–1977*. San Francisco: Ignatius Press, 1998.

———. *Salt of the Earth: The Church at the End of the Millennium*. San Francisco: Ignatius Press, 1997.

Ratzinger, Joseph, and Vittorio Messori. *The Ratzinger Report: An Exclusive Interview on the State of the Church*. San Francisco: Ignatius Press, 1985.

Tobin, Greg. *Holy Father: Benedict XVI, Pontiff for a New Era*. New York: Sterling Publishing, 2005.

FURTHER READING AND WEBSITES

BOOKS

Allen, John L. *The Rise of Benedict XVI: The Inside Story of How the Pope Was Elected and Where He Will Take the Catholic Church*. New York: Doubleday, 2005.

Bardazzi, Marco. *In the Vineyard of the Lord: The Life, Faith, and Teachings of Joseph Ratzinger, Pope Benedict XVI*. New York: Rizzoli International, 2005.

Behnke, Alison. *Pope John Paul II*. Minneapolis: Twenty-First Century Books, 2006.

Benedict XVI. *Truth and Tolerance: Christian Belief and World Religions*. San Francisco: Ignatius Press, 2004.

————. *The Yes of Jesus Christ*. New York: Crossroad Publishing Company, 2005.
Greeley, Andrew M. *The Making of the Pope 2005*. New York: Little Brown and Company, 2005.
Weigel, George. *God's Choice: Pope Benedict XVI and the Future of the Catholic Church*. New York: HarperCollins, 2005.

WEBSITES

Cardinal Ratzinger: Pope Benedict XVI
http://www.crossroadsinitiative.com/library_author/114/Cardinal_Ratzinger.html
This site offers a brief biography and photos of Pope Benedict XVI and links to selected works.
The Holy See: Pope Benedict XVI
http://www.vatican.va/holy_father/benedict_xvi/index.htm
This site has links to the Vatican television center, where you can get a live view inside the grounds of the Vatican. Viewers can also read a biography of Pope Benedict XVI and many of his messages, apostolic letters, encyclicals, and letters. The site also shows the pope's coat of arms in detail and explains the symbolism. Text from audiences he has held and homilies and speeches he has given are posted. There is also a photo gallery and a map of the Vatican city state.
The Life of Pope Benedict XVI
http://www.ewtn.com/pope/life/index.asp
A biography of Pope Benedict XVI and his namesake are provided on this site, as well as an explanation of the symbols on the pope's coat of arms.
The Pope Benedict XVI Fan Club
http://www.popebenedictxvifanclub.com/
The home page of this site offers basic information about Pope Benedict XVI. The site contains an archive of Cardinal Ratzinger's articles, correspondence, and spoken addresses. It contains interviews, articles, and commentary about the pope, selected addresses and writings, and his first encyclical. In the future, it will archive mainly his written works as pope.
The Pope Blog: Pope Benedict XVI
http://thepopeblog.blogspot.com/

This site is an unofficial blog covering Pope Benedict XVI. It provides links to archives and headline stories.
Profile: Pope Benedict XVI.
    http://news.bbc.co.uk/1/hi/world/europe/4445279.stm
    A profile on Pope Benedict is offered on this site provided by the British Broadcasting Corporation (BBC) news department. Key stories are posted as well as background information on various issues, world reaction to the pope's election, videos, and news related to Benedict XVI.
Vatican: The Holy See
    http://www.vatican.va/
    This site offers a vast collection, including a resource library, daily news bulletins, a photo gallery, and historic archival information. Visitors to this site will also find an amazing virtual tour of beautiful paintings and a sea of papal and historic documents and events. This site is the closest thing to a tour of the Vatican—well worth a visit.

WEBSITES

Website addresses in this book were valid at the time of printing. However, because of the nature of the Internet, some addresses may have changed or sites may have closed since publication. While the author and Publisher regret any inconvenience this may cause readers, no responsibility for any such changes can be accepted by the author or Publisher.

INDEX

OTHER TITLES FROM LERNER AND BIOGRAPHY®:

Ariel Sharon
Arnold Schwarzenegger
The Beatles
Benito Mussolini
Benjamin Franklin
Bill Gates
Billy Graham
Carl Sagan
Che Guevara
Chief Crazy Horse
Colin Powell
Daring Pirate Women
Edgar Allan Poe
Eleanor Roosevelt
Fidel Castro
Frank Gehry
George Lucas
George W. Bush
Gloria Estefan
Hillary Rodham Clinton
Jacques Cousteau
Jane Austen
Jesse Ventura
J. K. Rowling
Joseph Stalin
Latin Sensations

Legends of Dracula
Legends of Santa Claus
Malcolm X
Mao Zedong
Mark Twain
Maya Angelou
Mohandas Gandhi
Napoleon Bonaparte
Nelson Mandela
Osama bin Laden
Pope Benedict XVI
Queen Cleopatra
Queen Elizabeth I
Queen Latifah
Rosie O'Donnell
Saddam Hussein
Stephen Hawking
Thurgood Marshall
Tiger Woods
Tony Blair
Vladimir Putin
Wilma Rudolph
Winston Churchill
Women in Space
Women of the Wild West
Yasser Arafat

ABOUT THE AUTHOR

Tom Streissguth lives in Florida and works as a writer and editor. He has written more than fifty books for young people, including biographies and books on history. His volumes in the BIOGRAPHY® series include *Legends of Dracula* and *Queen Cleopatra*. Tom has also written a short children's novel, *Mystery at the Great Wall*.

PHOTO ACKNOWLEDGMENTS

The images in this book are used with the permission of: © Franco Origlia/Getty Images, p. 2; © Joe Raedle/Getty Images, p. 6; © Jan Pitman/Getty Images, p. 10; © Keystone/Getty Images, pp. 17, 20, 40, 59; © German Catholic News Agency KNA via Getty Images, p. 18; © Franziska Krug/Action Press/ZUMA Press, pp. 26, 54; © Reuters, p. 29; © Arte & Immagini srl/CORBIS, p. 31; © KNA-BILD/Action Press/ZUMA Press, p. 32; © age fotostock/SuperStock, p. 34; Library of Congress, p. 37 (LC-DIG-ppmsca-00787); © Ric/Colorise/ZUMA Press, p. 39; © KNA/MAXPPP/ZUMA Press, p. 44; © Fox Photos/Getty Images, p. 46; © Bettmann/CORBIS, pp. 49, 53; © EPA/CORBIS, p. 56; © Frank Leonhardt/EPA/CORBIS, p. 60; © Gerard Malie/AFP/Getty Images, p. 64; © Mike Persson/AFP/Getty Images, p. 68; © MedioImages/Getty Images, p. 71; © Gabriel Bouys/AFP/Getty Images, p. 72; © Michael Springer/Getty Images, p. 75; © Jodi Hilton/Getty Images, p. 76; © Robert Willett/News-Observer/ZUMA Press, p. 81; © Michel Gangne/AFP/Getty Images, p. 82; © Maurizio Brambatti/AFP/Getty Images, p. 86; © Marco Longari/AFP/Getty Images, p. 89; © Arturo Mari-Pool/Getty Images, p. 90; © Vincenzo Pinto/AFP/Getty Images, p. 94; © Peter Edwards/Toronto Star/ZUMA Press, p. 99; © Getty Images, p. 101; © Pier Paolo Cito/AFP/Getty Images, p. 103.

Front cover: © Federico Gambarini/Pool/Reuters/CORBIS.
Back cover: © KNA-BILD/Action Press/ZUMA Press.